LETTER TO

MY

NON-CATHOLIC

FRIEND

LETTER TO MY NON-CATHOLIC FRIEND

CATHOLIC TREASURES
1823 Business Center Drive
Duarte, California 91010
USA

CATHOLIC TREASURES
1823 Business Center Drive
Duarte, California 91010
USA

www.catholictreasures.com
orders2@catholictreasures.com

ISBN 1-885692-13-7

September 24, 1991
Feast of Our Lady of Ransom

My Dear Friend,

More than likely, if you have managed to keep your sanity
in today's sad and sinful world, you may have been
scandalized even at what has been happening in the
Catholic Church. At the present time, she seems to have
fallen prey to all the snares of Satan set to trap not only
the weakest of men but also the most brilliant of
theologians.

How is it, you may well ask, that as a Catholic I can still
profess allegiance to my Church? With the help of our dear
Lord, and that of His most blessed Mother, I will try to
explain. To begin with:

THE CATHOLIC CHURCH WAS FOUNDED
DIRECTLY BY CHRIST

In the Old Testament the Jewish Tabernacle was the work
of God – not man. It was God who drew up its plan, giving
its exact dimensions, stipulating the materials to be used in
its construction, describing its sacred furnishings and
vessels for the service, and the vestments and ornaments
for the priests who would minister therein. He gave it a
suitable constitution, appointed its rulers, and defined the
extent of their power. (See Book of Exodus, chapters 25
through 31, entire Book of Leviticus; Book of Numbers,
chapters 1, 3 through 8, and 17 and 18.) So, since the
Tabernacle of the *Old* Law (which was but a *shadow*, a
figure, of the Church to come) was the work of God, surely
the Church of the *New* Testament (the *substance*, the
reality) must likewise be the work of God.

It is easily shown that it was Christ Himself, not His
followers, not even His Apostles, who established the

Church: Christ declared His *intention* of founding a Church, by the institution of a living authority, when He said to Simon Peter: "Thou art Peter, and upon this rock I will build My Church, and the gates of hell shall not prevail against it" (Matt. 16:18). Now, if Christ intends personally to build His Church, it is not to be the work of man. Christ Himself will therefore give it all the necessary elements of a true social body, and, consequently, a ruling authority. And, that there might be no room for doubt, He added: "And I will give to thee the keys of the kingdom of heaven. Whatsoever thou shalt bind upon earth, it shall be bound also in heaven; and whatsoever thou shalt loose on earth, it shall be loosed also in heaven" (Matt. 16:19). This authority was *actually established* and the Church founded, when Our Lord after His resurrection said to Peter: "Feed My lambs; feed My sheep" (John 21:15,17). During His mortal life Christ Himself was the visible head of the infant Church, but after His Resurrection the office of visibly feeding the flock was to be discharged by another, to whom Christ gave the necessary authority and office. And as the followers of the law of Moses under the Old Testament formed one compact body, so too were the followers of Christ to be One Body: "One Lord, one faith, one baptism" (Ephesians 4:5). From the moment when first the Church, after the descent of the Holy Ghost, appeared before the world, we find a compact, fully organized society, with the apostles at its head. "They, therefore, who received his (Peter's) word were baptized; and there were added in that day about three thousand souls. And they were persevering in the doctrine of the apostles, and in the communication of the breaking of bread, and in prayers" (Acts of the Apostles, 2:41,42).

It was by the preaching of the apostles, it is true, that the faithful were gained for the Church; but it was not the apostles who devised the plan of this body, made baptism the condition of membership, appointed the first supreme head, and invested him with authority. It was Christ Himself who did all this, and by so doing founded the Church. A "church of the future" is, therefore, no less absurd than a Christian religion of the future, for the founder of the Christian religion was at the same time the immediate founder of the Church. Being outside the Church was considered by the early Church Fathers as being a non-Christian. "He is no Christian," says St. Cyprian (died 258), "who is not within the Church of Christ" (Ep. ad Antonian, 55, n.24).

CHRIST ESTABLISHED A VISIBLE CHURCH

In the New Testament we learn that Christ was visibly on earth but a very short time; that the term of His public teaching comprised only three years, which was occupied chiefly with the instruction of twelve men, who, under a chief, were to constitute His first representative corporate teaching body; they would be commissioned by the Son of God to "go forth and teach all nations" in His name (Matt. 28:18,19). They would have successors in office, since the Kingdom of Christ was not only to be world-wide, but would endure until the end of time: "of His Kingdom there shall be no end" (Luke 1:33). And though Jesus would return to Heaven, He would not be disassociated from His visible teaching body: "Behold, I am with you all days, even unto the consummation of the world" (Matt. 28:20). If men employ every means in their power for the perpetuation of their work, can we imagine that God left His great work to drift along unguided and unprotected? If the Bible teaches anything plainly it is the visibility of Christ's Church. It is composed of rulers and subjects: "Take heed to yourselves and to the whole flock in which the Holy Spirit has placed you as bishops to rule the Church of God, which He has purchased with His own blood" (Acts 20:28). Its members are admitted by a visible external rite (Baptism); they must hear, and obey: "He who hears you, hears Me; he who rejects you, rejects Me" (Luke 10:16). Christ compares His Church only to things visible: a "flock" (John 21:15-17), "a sheepfold" (John 10:16), a "city seated on a mountain" (Matt. 5:14), a "kingdom" (Matt. 13). He calls it "My

4

Church" (Matt. 16:18), (not *"Churches"*), *"The* Church"
(Matt. 18:17). Fittingly, then, does this Kingdom of God
upon earth merit the designation of St. Paul: "The
Church of the living God" (1 Tim 3:15).

Pope Pius XI in an encyclical of January 6, 1928 on
"Fostering True Religious Unity" states: "The Church
thus wonderfully instituted could not cease to exist with
the death of its Founder and of the Apostles, the pioneers of
its propagation, for its mission was to lead all men to
salvation without distinction of time or place. 'Going
therefore, teach ye all nations' (Matt. 28:19). Nor could the
Church ever lack the effective strength necessary for the
continued accomplishment of its task, since Christ Himself
is perpetually present with it, according to His
promise: 'Behold, I am with you all days, even to the
consummation of the world' (Matt. 28:20). Hence not only
must the Church still exist today and continue always to
exist, but it must ever be exactly the same as it was in the
days of the Apostles. Otherwise we must say – which God
forbid – that Christ has failed in His purpose, or that He
erred when He asserted of His Church that the gates of hell
should never prevail against it" (Matt. 16:18).

Forty-seven times the word "Church" is found in the Old
Testament, and in each passage it means but *one* Church,
one way of worshipping the Lord before the coming of
Christ. That was the Jewish Church – the religion and the
law of Moses established by God. From no other altars did
God receive the sacrifice of prayer. They were all
abominations to Him. "He who turneth away his ears from
hearing the law, his prayer shall be an abomination"
(Proverbs 28:9). In the New Testament, twenty-four times
"the Church" is mentioned in the Acts of the Apostles, and
you find but one Church mentioned. Sixty-eight times St.
Paul speaks of "the Church" in his Epistles, everywhere
meaning but the one Church of God. St. John speaks of
"the Church at Ephesus," "at Smyra," "at Philadelphia,"
etc., but these were different dioceses. They all belonged to
the Catholic Church under Peter.

CHRIST FOUNDED AN APOSTOLIC
TEACHING BODY

After Christ appointed Apostles to carry on the work He had begun, He bade them go and teach all nations, baptizing those who would believe, and teaching them to observe whatsoever He had commanded. The Apostles were sent, not as mere messengers, but as ambassadors bearing Christ's authority and power, and teaching and ministering in His name and person; so that in hearing them men were hearing Him, and in despising them they were despising Him (Matt. 28:18-20; Luke 10:16). In order that they might carry out this commission, Christ promised them the Spirit of Truth. "I will ask the Father, and he shall give you another Paraclete, that he may abide with you forever. The spirit of truth, whom the world cannot receive, because it seeth him not, nor knoweth him: but you shall know him; because he shall abide with you, and shall be in you. He will teach you all things, and bring all things to your mind, whatsoever I shall have said to you" (John 14:16,17,26). Finally, He promised to be with them, not for a few years or a generation, but for all days, thereby indicating that the apostolic order should last beyond the lives of its present members, even to the end of time. "Behold I am with you all days, even to the consummation of the world" (Matt. 28:20). In thus constituting the apostolic body, Christ was in reality constituting His Church. The Church was no mere collection of individual believers, but a definite organization, which was to be the pillar and ground of truth: "I write these things to thee hoping to come to thee shortly, but in order that thou mayest know, if I am delayed, how to conduct thyself in *the house of God*, which is *the Church of the living God, the pillar and mainstay of the truth*" (1 Tim. 3:14,15). It was to be founded on a rock. "Thou art Peter; and upon this rock I will build My Church" (Matt. 16:18). The Church taken as a whole comprises teachers and believers, but its essential constitution lies in the existence of a teaching authority, guaranteed by Christ to be *infallible*. "Thou art Peter; and upon this rock I will build My Church, *and the gates of hell shall not prevail against it*" (Matt. 16:18).

Such was the original constitution of the Church; and as the Church was to last for all ages, it is natural to suppose that it should always continue to exist according to its original constitution – that is to say, as an apostolic teaching body. There are no signs that this organization was a temporary expedient, to die out after a few years and leave a totally different system in its place. He did not say to His Apostles: "Lo! I am with you even to the end of your *lives*;" but "Lo! I am with you all days, *even to the consummation of the world.*" So that those to whom he addressed himself were to live to the end of the world! What does this mean, but that the Apostles were to have successors, in whom their rights were to be perpetuated? Successors whom Jesus would ever assist by His presence and uphold by His power. The work founded by a *God*, out of His love for man, and at the price of His own precious Blood, must surely be imperishable!

PETER IS MADE CHIEF SHEPHERD OF CHRIST'S CHURCH; THE POPES SUCCEED PETER

The unique place of primacy Peter enjoyed among Jesus' apostles is especially evident from three Bible texts: Matt. 16:13-19; Luke 22:31 sqq., and John 21:15 sqq. The first passage tells us how our Savior changed Peter's name, by calling him "Kepha," the Aramaic word for "rock," which in Latin is "petros," from which derives the English "Peter." So "Peter" means "rock." (Formerly he had been known as "Simon.") By this symbolic act, the Lord meant to designate Peter as the foundation of the Church He intended to establish; Peter was to be the sign of stability, permanence, and unity. In this same passage, moreover, Peter is promised both the keys to heaven's Kingdom and the power to bind and to loose. Luke 22:24-32 is the text relating a controversy among the disciples. On this occasion Christ foretold that Peter was about to be put to the test by Satan: "Simon, Simon, behold Satan hath desired to have you, that he may sift you as wheat" (Luke 22:31). This test occurred, of course, at the hour of Calvary. "I tell you, Peter . . . that the cock shall not crow today, until you have three times denied that you know Me" (Luke 22:34). But the prayer of Christ, said for Peter in particular, would save him, so that he in turn might "confirm his brethren" in faith: "But I have prayed for thee, that thy faith fail not: and thou, being once converted, confirm thy brethren" (Luke 22:32). Again, therefore, Peter is the rock and bulwark of the faith. In John 21:15 sqq., Jesus fulfills His pledge to give Peter the keys of heaven. This is the beautiful passage in which Peter is made shepherd of Christ's universal flock. The Acts of the Apostles show us how Peter functioned in his role of chief shepherd. He is the primary spokesman for the apostles; even though we read of Peter's "standing with the Eleven," it is Peter who speaks. He is the principal preacher, the pacesetter for apostolic endeavor. Read, for example, Acts 1:15-26; 2:14-40; 3:1-26; 4:8; 5:1-11; 5:29; 8:14-17; etc. That Peter eventually went to Rome – clearly through the Spirit's guidance – is the testimony of St. Ignatius of Antioch (died 107), as well as several other ancient chroniclers. As early as the first century, too, Pope St. Clement I, a successor of Peter in Rome (even though St. John the Apostle still lived), demonstrates possession of full responsibility for the whole Church in a dispute involving the Corinthians. Tertullian and Hippolytus, both second-century witnesses, acknowledge Peter as the first in the succession of Bishops of Rome; St. Cyprian, in the third century, views the unity of the Church as originating from Peter. And from the second century on, the Bishop of Rome was asked for judgment in controversial ecclesial issues. (St. Peter and St. Paul's relics are in St. John Lateran Basilica in Rome.)

8

THE APOSTOLIC TEACHING BODY CONTINUES
TO THE PRESENT DAY

Passing through the ages, we find the same Apostolic system of teaching. Down to the sixteenth century, there existed in Christendom no other than this idea. The Bishops were looked upon as successors of the Apostles, and their unanimous teaching under the Pope was regarded as absolutely trustworthy – as truly representing the doctrine of Christ. The Church as a whole could not possibly fall into error – this was guaranteed by the promises of Christ: "The gates of hell shall not prevail against it" (Matt 16:18); and those who claimed scripture in support of new doctrines, and against the prevailing doctrine of the Church, were regarded as heretics and rebels against Christ, and against His authority delegated to the Church.

THE CHURCH CAME TO BE KNOWN AS
THE "CATHOLIC" CHURCH

The following is quoted from the book "Outlines of European History" by James Breasted and James Robinson, copyright 1914, which was used as a textbook at Classen Public High School in Oklahoma City in the 1930's. (So it is not a *Catholic* school history book.): "It was not until about the third century that Christians came to call their Church 'Catholic' (meaning 'universal'). The Catholic Church embraced all true believers in Christ, wherever they might be. To this one universal Church all must belong who hoped to be saved" (page 308). And then it quotes St. Cyprian (died 258) as follows: "Whoever separates himself from the Church is separated from the promises of the Church . . . He is an alien, he is profane, he is an enemy; he can no longer have God for his father who has not the Church for his mother. If any one could escape who was outside the Ark of Noah, so also may he escape who shall be outside the bounds of the Church." (Note: Breasted & Robinson's text errs, however, as to the date the Church came to be called "Catholic." St. Ignatius of Antioch (died 107) called the Church "Catholic" in his writings.)

So until the Sixteenth Century when Martin Luther broke away from the Catholic Church, the overwhelming majority of Christians were Roman Catholics.

THE PROTESTANT REBELLION

The Protestant rebellion continues to be in fact what its adherents call it today – a protest, and themselves Protest-ants, Protestants. A protest against what? *Against Christ's divinely constituted teaching authority in the world – His Church –* and the substitution of the Bible, interpreted by each individual, in its place. This ran counter to the almost unanimous conviction of Christendom for fifteen hundred years!

WHAT WERE THE CAUSES OF THE PROTESTANT REBELLION?

First, there had been a gradual relaxation of discipline which had weakened authority and opened the way to many scandals and unpunished abuses in the ranks of the clergy. "At the close of the Middle Ages and dawn of the new era, the Papacy had been too eager in the pursuit of humanistic aims, had cultivated too exclusively merely human ideals of art and learning, and at the same time had become entangled in secular business and politics, and was altogether too worldly" (Grisar, "LUTHER", V. p. 427). Moreover, in Germany at this time the Bishops were mostly younger sons of princely or noble houses who were quite unfitted for their spiritual work. And as for the lower clergy, secular and religious, while many were zealous to diffuse religious knowledge by catechetical teaching, sermons, instructive publications and educational work in the elementary and middle schools, many others were quite neglectful of these sacred duties.

So there were abuses in the Church then, as there are today, and as there always will be. But "Blessed is he who shall not be scandalized in Me" (Luke 7:23). Christ did not guarantee His Church from *scandal*, but from *error*: "When He, the Spirit of truth, has come, He will teach you *all truth*" (John 16:13). There were scandals in the Church even while Jesus was with it. Judas was a thief, a traitor, and a suicide; Peter, the head, swore to a falsehood; James and John quarreled over supremacy; St. Peter and St. Paul were at variance over circumcision, and St. Paul excommunicated one of the faithful for unspeakable lust. The Church is made up of *men*, not *angels*. The triumph of the Church is not in being composed of sinless mortals, but in supplying sinful men with means to carry on the struggle against their vicious tendencies. But Jesus by His divine power granted that His Church, even though composed of weak and sinful men, would never teach *error*. The Church may have needed house cleaning in the sixteenth century, but the way to clean house is not to dynamite it. A child may have a very dirty face and yet be absolutely pure in body and soul. "I am black but beautiful," sings the Church to all men in the words of Solomon (Canticles 1:4); that is, although the Catholic Church, the very Body of Jesus Christ in time and space, may appear to the eyes of men as it were black and contemptible; but inwardly, that is, in its faith and morals, fair and beautiful in the eyes of God.

You cannot heal a diseased member of the body by cutting it off. Cut away a member of the body from the heart's blood, and it dies. The spark of life animating the body does not follow the severed member. The spark of life remains with the body, and the severed member begins to disintegrate and decay. This is precisely what happened to the followers of the revolution of the sixteenth century, as we shall soon see. "It follows that those who are divided in faith and in government cannot be living in one Body . . . and cannot be living the life of its one divine Spirit" (Encyclical of Pope Pius XII, "The Mystical Body of Christ").

No people can form by themselves a congregation or church, claiming that they follow the teachings of Christ. Christ did not say: "Thou art Luther and upon this rock I will build my Church" (or "Thou art Calvin, Knox, King Henry VIII," etc.). Numberless are the false churches. "Among you there will be lying teachers who will bring in destructive sects . . . and many will follow . . . " (2 Peter 2:1,2) . . . "and by pleasing speeches, and good words, seduce the hearts of the innocent" (Romans 16:18). "In the last times, some shall depart from the faith, giving heed to spirits of error and doctrines of devils . . . " (1 Tim. 4:1-2); "For there shall be a time, when they will not endure sound doctrine: but according to their own desires, they will heap to themselves teachers, having to themselves itching ears: and will turn away their hearing from the truth" (2 Tim. 4:3-4). "They received not the love of truth that they might be saved. Therefore God shall send them the operation of error, to believe lying" (2 Thess. 2:10-11). "There is a way that *seemeth* just to a man, but the ends thereof lead to death" (Proverbs 14:12).

CAUSE OF THE RAPID SPREAD AND ESTABLISHMENT OF PROTESTANTISM

How was it possible that the Revolution became so widespread in such a short period of time, and that whole nations gave up the faith of their forefathers? One cause which greatly contributed to the defection was that the civil rulers in Germany, Scandinavia, England, and elsewhere, took advantage of the disorder, seeing in the rebellion a coveted opportunity of gaining absolute control over the people and of confiscating the property of the Church; and they gave to the leaders of the rebellion a

support without which the revolt everywhere would have
failed utterly.

The traitorous political ambition of France helped set up
Protestantism permanently in Europe. It was Cardinal
Richelieu (1585-1642), Prime Minister and real ruler of
France under Louis XIII, who, to ensure the political
victory of France in Europe, took the side of the Protestant
princes of Germany against the Catholic Emperor,
Ferdinand II, at the most critical moment of the Thirty
Years' War between the forces of Protestantism and
Catholicism. Cardinal Richelieu hired the Protestant
military genius, Gustavus Adolphus, for five tubs of gold, to
enter the war against the Catholics. The defeat of
Ferdinand made impossible his dream of a Europe united
again as one family by the Faith, so close to realization but
for the treachery of the French Cardinal.

Another cause was the popular unrest and love of novelty
which characterized the sixteenth century, and the
discontent and evil elements that are present at all times
in every society. Furthermore, the recent invention of
printing enabled the Protestants to circulate their
teachings, thus confusing and deceiving the minds of
simple folk.

THE CATHOLIC COUNTER-REFORMATION

Long before the Protestant revolt, all serious-minded
Catholic men and women were convinced that a
purification of the Church in her hierarchy and in her
members was needed. Not the Catholic *religion*, as the
Protestants maintained, but the *people* who professed that
religion required reformation. "Men must be changed by
religion," as one of the champions of true reform remarked,
"not religion by men." Our Lord told us not to be
scandalized when we see "cockle and wheat in His Church"
(Matt. 13:24-30). But why blame the Church for bad

Catholics? All the bad Catholics in the world are not the Catholic Church. The Catholic Church holds the "deposit of Faith," spoken of by St. Paul (1 Tim. 6:20-21). The bad Catholics are bad not because of being Catholic, but because they neglect their Catholic duties and disgrace their exalted condition. "The Church is a *perfect* body, composed of *imperfect* men. This is the mystery of faith which is a stumbling block to those outside it" (St. Augustine).

So the first goal of the counter-reformation was the purification of the Church in her hierarchy, and in her members. The spread of error by Protestants, who attacked the Divine Constitution of the Church and her fundamental doctrines, also imposed upon the Catholic leaders the duty of setting forth in unmistakable and authoritative terms the true doctrine of Christianity contained in Scripture and Tradition. For this purpose, an ecumenical council was convened (The Council of Trent, the Nineteenth Council of the Church) in the year 1545. The Council set up a vast program to restore religious discipline, revive Faith, and check the spread of Protantism by defining dogmatically the doctrines under attack and censuring the errors of the rebellion.

There is no better proof for the divine origin and guidance of the Church than the fact that she not only survived the great Protestant Revolt of the Sixteenth Century, but emerged from the conflict rejuvenated and prepared to meet new ones.

With regard to the teachings of the "reformers":

WHICH WAS APPOINTED BY CHRIST TO TEACH MANKIND THE TRUE RELIGION – THE CHURCH OR THE BIBLE?

When our Divine Saviour sent His Apostles throughout the world to preach the Gospel to every creature, He laid down the conditions of salvation thus: "He who believeth and is baptized shall be saved, but he who believeth not shall be condemned" (Mark 16:16). Here, then, our Blessed Lord laid down two absolute and universal conditions – Faith and Baptism. What is this Divine Faith which we must have in order to be saved? It is to believe, *upon the authority of God*, "all things whatsoever" (Matt: 28:20) He has revealed. Therefore if a man would be saved he must profess the *true* Religion. Now if God commands me under pain of damnation to believe what He has taught, He is bound to give me the means to know what He has taught. What is this means?" "The Bible," say the Protestants. But we Catholics say, "No, not the Bible, but the Church of God." For if God had intended that man should learn his religion from the Bible, surely God would have given that book to man. But He did not do so. Christ sent His apostles throughout the earth and said: "Go ye therefore, and teach all nations, baptizing them in the name of the Father, and of the Son, and of the Holy Ghost, teaching them to observe all things whatsoever I have commanded you" (Matt. 28:19,20). Christ did not say, sit down and write Bibles, and then let every man read and judge for himself. Since the sixteenth century we have seen the result of such thinking in the founding of hundreds of religions by men, all quarreling with one another about the interpretation of the Bible. Jesus never wrote a line of scripture nor did He command His Apostles to do so, except when He directed St. John to write the Apocalypse (Book of Revelations 1:11), but ordered them to "teach all nations" (Matt. 28:19). In Matt. 18:17, He does not say, "He who will not read the scriptures," but "he who will not hear the Church, let him be to thee as the heathen and the publican." The Apostles never circulated a single volume of scripture, but going forth, preached everywhere (Mark 16:20). It is true that our Lord said on one occasion, "Search the Scriptures for in them ye think ye have eternal life, and the same are they that give testimony of me" (John 5:39). This passage is quoted by Protestants in favor of private interpretation but proves nothing of the kind. Our Saviour speaks here only of the *Old* Testament, because the New Testament was not yet written. He addressed, not the Apostles, but the Pharisees, and reproaches them for not admitting His Divinity, clearly known and shown by the prophets of the Old Testament.

The Church established by Christ existed about 65 years before St. John wrote the last book of the Bible. During these years how did the people know what they had to do to save their souls? Was it from the Bible they learned it? No, because the Bible as such was not yet composed. They knew it precisely as we know it, from the teaching of the Church of God. The New Testament writings were not gathered together and declared to be divinely inspired until late in the fourth century. Moreover, these witnesses were Catholics, and accepted the Scriptures as divinely inspired because their Church declared them to be so. Protestants hold that the writings, known as the Sacred Scriptures, are inspired. But it is on the Catholic Church's word that they hold this truth! They take for granted that followers of the Catholic Church transcribed and translated the original writings without making any errors, that they never altered a line, that they preserved them until the sixteenth century in their original purity and integrity. Unless they grant all this, they cannot logically appeal to the Scriptures as divine authority. Thus Protestants are breaking away from their theory of "Nothing but the Bible" and basing their arguments on Tradition, or on the authority of the Catholic Church, which, on principle, they repudiate!

The Jewish religion existed before the Old Testament was written, just as the Christian Church existed before the New Testament was written. Peter converted three thousand before the first word of the New Testament was put on paper. Paul had converted hundreds of Romans, Corinthians, Galatians and Thessalonians before he wrote his epistles to those congregations; and all the Apostles were dead, and millions had died Catholic martyrs, before St. John wrote the last part of the New Testament. Until the end of the first century the "Word of God" could have been delivered only by *word of mouth.*

HOW THE APOSTLES REGARDED
THE NEW TESTAMENT

The Apostles seem to think it an important matter to leave us their recollections of Christ's life and character, but they make no pretense of giving us a complete written account of His teaching. They show no signs of regarding it as a duty to leave behind them full written particulars. St. John himself declares the impossibility of writing anything like an exhaustive account of all that Christ did (John 21:25). As far as we can gather, nearly all the Apostles were dead or dispersed before half the New Testament was written. None of the Apostles ever saw the Gospel of St. John, except the author himself. Only St. John lived long enough to have seen the whole series which made up the New Testament; but there is no evidence to show that he actually did see it. The only clear reference made by one Apostle to another Apostle's writings is that of St. Peter, who tells us how hard St. Paul's epistles were to understand, *and how some had wrested them to their own destruction* (2 Peter 3:16). Scripture was regarded as a *witness* to the Church's teaching, not as a sole and adequate Rule of Faith to be substituted in its place.

ST. PAUL USED THE SCRIPTURES

In the Acts of the Apostles 17:2, we are told that St. Paul reasoned with the Thessalonians on three Sabbath days "out of the Scriptures," and in verse 11, Paul says that Bereans "searched the Scriptures." Verse 2 implies that St. Paul used the Bible and verse 11 that the Bereans had it; but this was not the *New* Testament, for very little of it had been written at that time. Read verse 3, and it will be clear that he was appealing to the prophetic writings of the *Old* Testament, showing them that Christ was to suffer and to rise again. He didn't prove from the Scriptures that Christ had already suffered. The same applies to verse 11.

THE FIRST CHRISTIANS WERE NOT "BIBLE" CHRISTIANS

The various parts which now make up the New Testament were carefully treasured and read in the local churches where they had been received, but it was only by degrees that copies were spread to other places and the whole came to be circulated throughout Christendom. It was late in the fourth century before the present New Testament writings were gathered together into one book. It was this late in the Christian era before the Catholic Church declared which of the many doubtfully inspired writings scattered throughout the world were really inspired.

HOW THE EARLY CHRISTIANS RECEIVED THEIR FAITH

We find in the New Testament many references to Christian doctrine as derived from *oral* teaching. The Thessalonians are told to "hold fast the traditions which they had been taught, whether by *word* or by epistle" (2 Thess. 2:15). Timothy, who had been ordained Bishop of Ephesus by St. Paul is instructed to "Hold fast the form of sound words which he had *heard* from his teacher among many witnesses"; "to continue in the things learnt" (that is, "the gospel which was committed to his trust"), "knowing from whom he had learnt them," "and to commit the same to faithful men who shall be able to teach others" (1 Tim. 1-11; 4:11-16; 6:20; 2 Tim 1:6, 13; 2:2, 3:10, 14; 4:2, etc.) – all of which certainly stands in favor of the Catholic doctrine of apostolic authority in a line of successors, for an *oral* transmission of Faith, and against the Protestant idea of substituting the Bible as the sole and adequate guide to salvation. The Bishops were universally regarded as the authoritative successors to the Apostles responsible for the preservation of Christian doctrine. The New Testament was not completed until 65 years after Peter and Paul and most of the other Apostles were dead; many of their immediate successors had been martyred, and it is likely that the third or fourth successors of the several Apostles were converting souls without the Bible when St. John completed his writings. In fact, the whole Roman Empire was Christian, at least ten million people remained true to Christ and suffered a martyr's death, and the Church was enjoying her golden age, before anybody ever saw the New Testament bound up into one volume. For four centuries people received their faith only by *hearing* it preached in Catholic churches.

Most Protestants enter the Protestant religion through family ties or evangelistic services – not by Bible reading. Very few people are led to embrace this or that religion by "searching the Scriptures." Nine times out of ten, they enter a religion first, and do their Bible reading afterwards.

The Bible was not given from Heaven like the Ten Commandments were – as the Christian's sole rule of faith; and Christ did not write the New Testament; and the Apostles were not ordered to write it as a text book. *Tradition* is also a rule of faith; for "Faith cometh by *hearing*" (Rom 10:17).

IS SCRIPTURE INHERENTLY CLEAR?

Suppose: an Episcopal minister reads the Bible in a prayerful spirit and says it is clear and evident that there must be "bishops." The Presbyterian, a sincere and well-meaning man, deduces from the Bible that there should be no bishops, only "Presbyters." A number of religions hold that baptism by immersion is correct, while others approve of baptism by sprinkling. Next comes the Unitarian who calls them all a pack of idolators, worshipping a man for a God, and he quotes several texts from the Bible to prove it. So we have here a number of denominations understanding the Bible in different ways. What then, if we bring together 500 denominations all differing? One says there is no hell; another says there is. One says Christ is God; another says He is not, etc. Is baptism necessary for salvation? Must infants be baptized? Are good works necessary, or is faith alone sufficient? The correct answer to these questions is surely essential, but zealous Bible readers do not agree concerning them. Is anyone foolish enough to believe that the changeless and eternal Holy Spirit is directing those five hundred denominations, telling one Yes and another No; declaring a thing to be black and white, false and true, at the same time? If the Bible were intended as the guide and teacher of man, would St. Peter have declared that "In the scriptures are things hard to be understood, which the unlearned and unstable wrest to their own destruction" (2 Peter 3:16)?

On the contrary, the Bible itself declares that it contains many passages, the meaning of which is not clear. Read Acts 8:27-35; Luke 24:25-27; 2 Peter 3:16. Moreover, if the Bible is the Protestants' authority for everything, how is it that they cannot quote the Bible in favor of the "private judgment" theory? Not only can it not be found, but you will find this declaration in the holy book: "No prophecy of Scripture is made by private interpretation" (2 Peter 1:20). St. Paul warned Titus not to concede to anyone the right of private judgment (Titus 3:9-11).

PRIVATE INTERPRETATION HAS MADE OF THE BIBLE A BABEL OF CONFUSION

Individual opinions have divided Christianity, and occasioned more infidelity than anything else. W. E. Lecky, in "RATIONALISM IN EUROPE," Vol. II, p. 174, states: "It has been most abundantly proved that from Scripture, honest and able men have derived and do derive arguments in support of the most opposite opinions." And from "The London Times" of January 13, 1884: "England alone is reputed to contain some 700 sects, each of which proves a whole system of theology and morals from the *Bible.*"

THE MAJORITY OF CHRISTIANS DID NOT HAVE THE BIBLE BEFORE THE FIFTEENTH CENTURY

Not only was the Bible not the Christian's written Rule of Faith during the first four centuries, but it was not during the next thousand years, for the simple reason that there was no widespread use of paper to print on until the thirteenth century, and the moveable-type printing press itself was not invented until the year 1450, more than one thousand years after the true canon of the Bible (the collection of books which were considered inspired) was determined. Without the printing presses, it was impossible to distribute Bibles by hundreds of thousands. It required several years of work, distributed over many hours of the day, to produce *one* copy of the Bible. Every page had to be handmade, with pen upon parchment. Who copied these Bibles by hand? In most monasteries, from the early centuries, the daily occupation of many thousands of monks consisted in copying the scriptures for the benefit of the world. Some excellent specimens exist, one of them now being displayed at the Congressional Library, in Washington, D.C. A copy of the manuscript-Bible was usually placed on a large table in church, where the people who could read might have the benefit of it. Some Protestant Churches spread the falsehood that the Catholic Church chained the Bible so that people might not learn anything from it. That is an anti-Catholic fable. The thick cover of the Bible was chained to the table (or podium) so that no one might steal the valuable work. In those days a

Bible would have cost over $10,000.00. The Bible was displayed in the church, wide-open, precisely that it might be read. Not one in 50,000 had a Bible. Would our Divine Lord have left the world for 1500 years without that book if it were necessary to man's salvation? Most assuredly not. But suppose everyone had Bibles? What good will that book be, even today, to the one-half of the people of the world who cannot read?

THE FIRST PROTESTANTS TOOK OUR BIBLE, NOT WE THEIRS

The printing press was invented 65 years before Luther's revolt; and according to Hallam, a Protestant historian, the Catholic Bible was the first book ever printed. In 1877 there were exhibited hundreds of old Bibles, at South Kensington, England; it was called the "Caxton Exhibition," and among them were nine German editions of the Bible, printed in Germany before Luther was born; and there were more than one hundred editions of the Latin Bible, the very thing Luther is pretended to have "discovered." This disproves the popular lie about Luther finding the Bible at Erfurt in 1507. Many Protestant historians have repudiated this charge. To name a few: Dr. McGilfert in MARTIN LUTHER AND HIS WORK, page 273, says: "If Luther was ignorant of the Bible, it was his own fault. The notion that Bible reading was frowned upon by ecclesiastical authorities of that age is quite unfounded." And Dr. Preserve Smith in LIFE AND LETTERS OF MARTIN LUTHER, page 14, writes: "The book was a very common one, there having been no less than one hundred editions of the Latin Vulgate published before 1500, as well as a number of German translations." And Murzel in HISTORY OF GERMANY, Vol. II, p. 223, says: "Before the time of Luther, the Bible had already been translated and printed in both High and Low Dutch."

OUR LORD SET UP A SUPREME COURT

When the Constitution of the United States was written, its writers did not leave it to the people to interpret as they saw fit. They knew better than that. They set up a Supreme Court for that purpose. And do you think that the all-wise God would be less careful in a matter of even greater importance where the salvation of millions of immortal souls is at stake? Most assuredly not. He, too, set up a "Supreme Court," to guide and teach His people, and to interpret the law for them. In the Old Testament, God chose Moses to deliver His people, the Israelites, from the Egyptians, and to rule over them during their 40 years of wandering in the desert towards the promised land. In the Book of Numbers, Chap. 27, verses 12-23, as the time of his death approaches, Moses asks God to "provide a man that may be over this multitude and may lead them out, or bring them in: lest the people of the Lord be as sheep without a shepherd. And the Lord said to him: Take Josue – a man in whom is the Spirit – and put thy hand upon him . . . and thou shalt give him precepts in the sight of all . . . that all the congregation of the children of Israel may hear him . . . he and all the children of Israel with him, and the rest of the multitude shall go out and go in *at his word.*" And in the Book of Deuteronomy, Moses was repeating and expounding to the Israelites the ordinances given on Mt. Sinai, with other precepts not expressed before. In Chapter 17, verses 8-12, he states: "If thou perceive that there be among you a hard and doubtful matter in judgment . . . and thou see that the words of the judges within thy gates do vary: arise, and *go up to the place, which the Lord thy God shall choose.* And thou shall come to the priests of the Levitical race, and to the judge that shall be at that time. And thou shalt ask of them. And they shall shew thee the truth of the judgment. And thou shalt do whatsoever they shall say, that preside in the place, which the Lord shall choose, and what they shall teach thee, according to His law. And thou shalt follow their sentence: *neither shalt thou decline to the right hand nor to the left hand.* But he that will be proud, and refuse to obey the commandment of the priest, who ministereth at that time to the Lord thy God (i.e., the high priest), and the decree of the judge: that man shall die . . ." And the footnote, Douay Bible, to this ordinance states: "Here we see what authority God was pleased to give to the church guides of the Old Testament, in deciding *without appeal*, all controversies relating to the law, *promising that they should not err therein*; and surely he has not done less for the church guides of the New Testament."

Christ set up that teaching organism called "the Church," with St. Peter and his successors as Chief Shepherd (that is, "high priest"), to be His official Custodian and interpreter under the New Law. And He promised to safeguard the Church from error. Read John 1:14; 14:6; 1 John 5:20; John 14:17; 15:26; 16:13; John 8:32; 17:17; 2 John 1:3. To that Church alone, and not to any *book* or *private individual* did He say "Teach ye all nations . . . I will be with you" (Matt. 28:20). And "He who will not hear *the Church*, let him be to thee as the heathen and the publican" (Matt. 18:17).

THE CATHOLIC CHURCH URGES ITS MEMBERS TO READ THE BIBLE

"At a time when a great number of bad books . . . are circulated among the unlearned . . . the faithful should be excited to the reading of the Bible; for this is the most abundant source which ought to be left open to every one to draw from it purity of morals and of doctrine" (Pope Pius VI, 1778). And Pope Leo XIII, elected in 1878, did much to promote the reading of the Holy Scriptures. He founded a congregation for the advancement of biblical studies; he addressed a letter to the whole Church on the subject of the reading and study of Holy Writ; and he granted special blessings to those who devoutly read the Holy Scriptures daily.

The Church authorities at the Synod of Oxford, in 1408, forbade the laity to read *unauthorized* versions of the Scriptures. In other words, she forbade them to accept as Scripture what really was not Scripture. For example, the Albigensians of the thirteenth century made a translation of the Bible which would square with their erroneous teachings. (See Hallam, MIDDLE AGES, Chapter IX). And Sir Thomas More says "Wycliffe took upon himself to translate the Bible anew. In this translation he purposely corrupted the holy text, maliciously planting in it such words as might, in the reader's ears, serve to prove such heresies as he 'went about to sow.' " (EVE OF THE REFORMATION, Gasquet, Chapter VIII). The Lollards changed the text still more, and made the Bible support the anarchy which they later preached throughout England.

HISTORY OF THE PROTESTANT ENGLISH BIBLE

"Tyndale's New Testament" was published under King Henry VIII; the "Bishop's Bible" in 1568; "The King James" or "Authorized Version" in 1611; "The Revised Version" in 1881. *Each of these was brought out because the previous one was found to contain errors.* (Read "History of the Reformation of the Church in England," by J. H. Blunt, Ch. I). Zwingli, writing to Luther, in commenting on his translation of the Bible into German, says: "Thou dost corrupt the word of God; thou art seen to be a manifest and common corrupter and perverter of the Holy Scriptures; how much are we ashamed of thee!" (Vol. II, DE SACRAMENTIS, p. 412). Here are some of his typical corruptions: "Wherefore, brethren," St. Peter commands us, "labor the more, that by good works you may make sure your vocation and election" (2 Peter 1:10); But Luther omitted the words "By good works." "We account a man to be justified by faith" (Romans 3:28). Luther added the word "alone." Calvin's translations of the Scriptures were equally faulty. A Protestant authority says: "Calvin makes the text of the gospel to leap up and down; he uses violence to the letter of the gospel, and besides this, adds to the text." (See Molinaeus' TRANSLATION OF THE NEW TESTAMENT, Part XI, p. 110). In his APOLOGY, Sec. 6, Mr. Burgess, a Protestant, says of the English Protestant version: "How shall I approve, under my hand, a translation which has many omissions, many additions; which sometimes obscureth, sometimes perverteth the sense, being sometimes senseless, sometimes contrary?"

So the prohibition of the Catholic Church against Bible-reading had reference to the reading of *faulty translations* of the Scriptures. Such faulty translations are not surprising, as the devil, too, quotes the Scriptures dishonestly: In Matthew 4:1-11, we read: "At that time, Jesus was led by the Spirit into the desert, to be tempted by the devil . . . Then the devil took Him up into the holy city, and set Him upon the pinnacle of the temple, and said to Him: if thou be the Son of God, cast thyself down. For it is written: That he hath given his angels charge over thee . . . " This we read in the 90th Psalm; but there the prophecy was not spoken of *Christ*, but of the *just man*; so the devil has quoted the Scriptures dishonestly. As Satan changes himself into an angel of light, and even from the Holy Scriptures prepares snares for Christians, so now he uses the testimonies of Scripture itself not to instruct, but to deceive.

THE CATHOLIC BIBLE CONTAINS MORE BOOKS THAN THE PROTESTANT BIBLE

Why? For the same reason that it contains any of the writings within its covers. As already explained, and no man in this world can refute it, the writings which the Protestants accept as inspired, they know to be so *only on the authority of the Catholic Church*. The Protestant Bible omits the following seven books from the Old Testament: Judith, Ecclesiasticus, Baruch, Tobias, Wisdom, and the two books of the Machabees. (Luther originally threw out 11 entire books!) These books are inspired Sacred Scripture, and for twenty centuries, from the compilation of the Old Testament canon by Esdras and Nehemias in 430 B.C., until the rebellion of the Protestants in the Sixteenth Century, they were accepted by the faithful as God's revelation to His people. They are still in the *Catholic* Bible.

Most of the Protestant and Catholic versions of the Bible have the same books in the New Testament. But the New Testament contains writings which were not written by the Apostles. Luke and Mark were not Apostles at all, and even Paul was not one of the original twelve. How could it possibly be proved, outside the Catholic Church's authority, that Mark's and Luke's writings were inspired? And how could one, rejecting this Church's authority, account for the omission of gospels written by St. Bartholomew and St. Thomas, and the acts of St. Andrew, who *were* apostles? Of these, several were regarded by certain of the Fathers as part of Scripture, and were publicly read in local Churches, while others in the second and third centuries classed them as doubtfully inspired. Likewise, the Epistle to the Hebrews, Revelations, James, Jude, 2nd Peter, and 2nd and 3rd John were at first called into question in some parts of the Church.

HOW THE CONTENTS OF THE NEW TESTAMENT WERE DETERMINED

So the collections of reputed inspired writings in different parts of Christendom in the second, third, and fourth centuries varied considerably, and it was at Church Councils at Hippo and Carthage (held between 393-419) that a list of authentic books was agreed upon. Pope Innocent I, and afterwards Pope Gelasius (A.D. 494), confirmed this list, and for the first time the New Testament was capable of being bound up into one book as we have it now. How was this question settled after so long a dispute? Purely and simply by an appeal to the traditions existing in local churches where each document had been preserved, and by the authoritative verdict of the Church, judging according to those traditions. Hence, the reliability of the Bible depends wholly on the authority of the *Roman Catholic Church*! Protestants, in accepting the New Testament as it stands, are acknowledging the authority of the Catholic Church in the fourth and fifth centuries, and some of them have candidly admitted this in writing. (See preface to Revised Version of Protestant Bible.)

HOW OLD ARE THE PROTESTANT CHURCHES?

The Lutheran Church was founded in the year 1517 by Martin Luther, a former priest of the Roman Catholic Church.

The Church of England (Anglicanism) was founded by King Henry VIII in 1534 when he threw off the authority of the Pope and proclaimed himself the head of the Church in England, because the Pope refused to declare invalid his marriage with Queen Catherine.

The Presbyterian denomination was begun in 1560 by John Knox who was dissatisfied with Anglicanism.

The Episcopalian denomination was begun in 1784 by Samuel Seabury who was dissatisfied with Presbyterianism.

The Baptist church was launched by John Smyth in Amsterdam, Holland in the year 1606.

The Methodist church was launched by John and Charles Wesley in England in 1744.

The Unitarians were founded by Theophilus Lindley in London, in 1774.

The Jehovah's Witness Church was developed in 1872 by Charles Russell.

The founder of The Salvation Army is William Booth, who quit the Anglicans, and then the Methodists, and set up his own version of Christianity in 1787. His own son, Ballinger, quit The Salvation Army and did the same for himself in 1896.

Mrs. Mary Baker Eddy began the Christian Scientist religion in 1879, basing it upon an outright denial of Original Sin and its effects.

The Mormon church, the Seventh-Day Adventists, the Church of Christ, The Church of the Nazarene, or any of the various Pentecostal Churches, etc. are also among the hundreds of new churches founded by *men* within the past few generations.

The Roman Catholic Church was founded by God-made-man, Jesus Christ, in the year 33 A.D. He said: "Thou art Peter, and upon this rock I will build My Church, and the gates of hell shall not prevail against it . . . Feed my lambs; feed My sheep" (Matt. 16:18,19; John 21:15,17). He also said: "He who is not with Me is against Me, and he who gathers not with me scatters" (Matt. 12:30).

MARTIN LUTHER

The Protestant Revolution was begun by Martin Luther, a Catholic priest, who, led astray by private judgment, set himself against the Faith held for 1500 years. He decided that all Christians before him had been in error. *Is it possible to believe that Jesus founded a Church to mislead the world, and then after 1500 years approved of over 500 contradictory churches founded by men?* But, you may say, the Protestant Church is the Church of Christ, purified of error, and only this purified form dates from Luther. I answer that you must choose between Luther and Christ. Jesus said His Church would never teach error (John 14:26); Luther says it did teach error. If Luther is right, Christ is wrong; if Christ is right, Luther and all his followers are wrong.

Luther's chief errors are contained in the following propositions: (1) There is no supreme teaching power in the Church. (2) The temporal sovereign has supreme power in matters ecclesiastical. (3) There are no priests. (4) All that is to be believed is in the Bible. (5) Each one may interpret Holy Scripture as he likes. (6) Faith alone saves, good works are superfluous. (7) Man lost his free will by original sin. (8) There are no saints, no Christian sacrifice, no sacrament of confession, no purgatory.

Following are some significant excerpts from Luther's writings and lectures, as compared with the teachings of our Lord Jesus Christ. (Taken from the book CHRIST VS. LUTHER, edited by R. A. Short, copyright 1953 by the Bellarmine Publishing Company, Mound, Minn.)

– On Sin –

Christ: "Now the works of the flesh are manifest, which are fornication . . . murder . . . and suchlike. And concerning these I warn you, they who do such things will not attain the Kingdom of God" (Galatians 5:19-21).

Luther: "Sin boldly but believe more boldly. Let your faith be greater than your sin . . . Sin will not destroy us in the reign of the Lamb, although we were to commit fornication a thousand times in one day" (Letter to Melanchton, August 1, 1521, Audin p. 178).

Christ: "And do not be drunk with wine, for in that is debauchery" (Eph. 5:18). "Keep thyself chaste" (I Tim. 5:22).

Luther: "Why do I sit soaked in wine? . . . To be continent and chaste is not in me" (Luther's diary).

– On Good Works –

Christ: "What will it profit, my brethren, if a man says he has faith, but does not have works?" "As the body without the spirit is dead, so faith without works is dead also" (James 2:14,26).
Luther: "He that says the Gospel requires works for salvation, I say, flat and plain, is a liar" (Table Talk, Weimer Edition, II, p. 137).

– On Truth –

Christ: "Do not be liars against the truth. This is not the wisdom that descends from above. It is earthly, sensual, devilish" (James 3:14-15). "Do not lie to one another" (Col. 3:9). "The Lord hateth . . . a lying tongue . . . a deceitful witness that uttereth lies . . . " (Proverbs 6:16-17). "A thief is worse than a liar, but both of them shall inherit destruction" (Ecclus. 20:27).
Luther: "To lie in case of necessity, or for convenience, or in excuse, would not offend God, who is ready to take such lies on Himself" (Eisenrach Conference, July 17, 1540).

– On Marriage –

Christ: "Whosoever shall put away his wife and marry another, committeth adultery against her. And if the wife shall put away her husband, and be married to another, she committeth adultery" (Mark 10:11-12).
Luther: "As to divorce, it is still a moot question whether it is allowable. For my part, I prefer bigamy" (DeWette, Vol. 2, p. 459).

– On Free Will –

Christ: "Woe to that man by whom the Son of Man is betrayed! It were better for that man if he had not been born" (Matt. 26:24). "Let no man say when he is tempted, that he is tempted by God; for God is no tempter to evil" (James 1:13).

Luther: "Judas' will was the work of God; God by His almighty power moved his will as He does all that is in this world" (De Servo Arbitro – Against man's free will). Accosted on all sides by charges of heresy, even by many of his former associates in the Protestant movement, Luther found refuge in this, the strangest of all his beliefs. No man is accountable for his actions, Luther taught, no matter how evil. Not even Judas!

Such are the teachings of the first so-called "reformer" of Christ's Church! If Luther was a man divinely inspired or called in an extraordinary manner, why did God permit him to fall into so many absurdities in points of doctrine?

"Luther finally brought himself to indulge the pleasing delusion that the Catholic Church was the detestable kingdom of Antichrist . . . that he himself was John the Evangelist . . . " (From the book LUTHER, P. 65).

So you see the heresies, divisions, confusion, etc. resulting from the private interpretation of the Scriptures. *Unless there is a church in the world, from the days of our Lord, which declares unmistakably (infallibly) who Jesus is, and what He taught, He might just as well have revealed nothing!*

CHRIST DID ESTABLISH SUCH A CHURCH, AND IT IS THE ROMAN CATHOLIC CHURCH

When Christ left us and ascended into Heaven, He gave His powers to the Church He had founded: "All power has been given Me by My Father; go then" (in virtue of this power that I delegate to you) "teach all nations to keep My commandments. He who hears you, hears Me; he who despises you, despises Me" (Matt. 28:18-20; Luke 10:16). So the Church is invested with the authority of Jesus Christ; she speaks and commands in Our Lord's name. The difference between Protestants and Catholics lies in the attitude of dependance on and of obedience to the living authority of the Church which teaches and governs in the name of Christ. The Catholic accepts the Church's doctrines, and regulates his conduct according to those doctrines, because he hears in the Church, and her head the Sovereign Pontiff, the voice of Christ. The Protestant admits a certain truth because he "discovers" it, or imagines himself to do so, by his personal lights. Claiming the right of private interpretation (despite 2 Peter 1:20; 3:16) and reading the Bible according to his reason alone, he takes or leaves what he will. Each one then, keeping his faculty of choosing, becomes his own sovereign pontiff. The Protestant *admits*; the Catholic *believes*. As soon as the Church speaks, the Catholic submits in all obedience as to Christ Himself. St. Isidore (Archbishop, Doctor, and Saint) stated: "We, as Catholics are not permitted to believe anything of our own will, nor to choose what someone has believed of his. We have God's apostles as authorities, *who did not themselves of their own wills choose anything of what they wanted to believe*, but faithfully transmitted to the nations, the teachings of Christ." In the Old Testament God spoke to the Israelites from the midst of the two Cherubim atop the Ark of the Covenant: "There will I give orders, and will speak to thee over the propitiatory, and from the midst of the two Cherubims, which shall be upon the Ark of the Testimony, all things which I will command the children of Israel . . . " (Exodus 25:22). Today He speaks to us through the Catholic Church. She, alone, speaks with His Voice.

THE CATHOLIC CHURCH CLAIMS TO BE INFALLIBLE IN HER TEACHINGS

In order to keep His Church in the truth, Christ sent His Spirit – the Spirit of Truth (John 14:17). "When the Spirit of truth is come, He will teach you all truth" (John 16:13); "He will teach you all things, and bring all things to your mind, whatsoever I shall have said to you" (John 14:26). (So nothing of what the divine Word spoke to men is to be lost)! "He will abide with you forever; and He shall be in you" (John 14:16,17). It is by the Holy Spirit, then, that the Church is ever to possess the truth, and nothing can rob her of it; for this Spirit, who is sent by the Father and the Son, will abide unceasingly *with* and *in* her.

The Holy Spirit is the principle of the Church's life. He makes Himself responsible for her words, just as *our spirit* is responsible for what our *tongue* utters. Hence it is that the Church, by her union with the Holy Spirit, is so identified with truth, that the apostle did not hesitate to call her "the pillar and ground of the truth" (1 Tim. 3:14-15). Consequently, the Church *has* to be infallible in her teaching; for how can she be deceived herself, or deceive others, seeing it is the Spirit of Truth who guides her in all things and speaks by her mouth? He is her soul; and when the tongue speaks, the soul is responsible.

The man who does not acknowledge the Church to be infallible, should, if he be consistent, admit that the Son of God has not been able to fulfil His promise, and that the Spirit of truth is a Spirit of error. He thought he was but denying a prerogative to the Church, whereas, in reality, he has refused to believe *God Himself*. It is this that constitutes the sin of heresy. Want of due reflection may hide the awful conclusion; but the conclusion is strictly implied in his principle.

In the year 52, all the Apostles came together at Jerusalem, under St. Peter, to talk over the affairs of the Church. This was the first Council of the Church, and the story of it is told in the Acts of the Apostles, Chapter 15. The Councils are an Apostolic institution, and the Apostles, when they instituted them, acted under the commission they received from Christ; otherwise they could not have published the decisions of their Council with the words, "It seemed good to the Holy Ghost and to us" (Acts 15:28).

The Apostles spoke with unerring authority, and their words were received not as human opinions, but as Divine Truths. "When you have received from us the word of God, you received it not as the word of *men*, but as the word of *God*" (1 Thess. 2:13).

THE POPE IS NOT INFALLIBLE IN ALL HIS ACTS

The President of the United States does not always act as President. No one would attribute presidential authority to his views on hunting, or yachting, or on drama. Even when he presides over a White House function he is not always using his presidential prerogatives. No one would attach the full authority of the United States Government to the remarks he makes to a deputation of Presbyterians, Jews, or Catholics. Even when speaking in a cabinet meeting, or making his official speech at the opening of Congress, he does not intend to throw the full weight of his authority into his utterances. It is only when signing an Act of Congress or a treaty with some foreign nation, that the full and highest exercise of his presidency comes into play. Then, and then alone, does he act as ruler of the Country, committing the Government to the deed, and binding the whole nation. As it is with the President of the United States, so it is with the Pope. In his private acts as a Christian or Bishop, or in his jurisdiction of the government of the Church, he might make a mistake or fail in prudence.

Therefore, the Bishop of Rome, the Pope, *can* make a mistake – unless he is speaking under certain conditions. These conditions are: (1) when he is speaking "ex cathedra" (from the Chair of Peter); and (2) manifests his intention of defining a doctrine (3) of faith or morals (4) officially binding the whole Church. At such a time the Pope's teaching is infallible; that is, at such a time he is assisted, watched over, by the Holy Spirit so that he does not use his authority and his knowledge to mislead the

Church. The Pope is not inspired; he receives no private revelations; he does not carry in his mind the whole of Christ's teaching as a miraculous treasure on which to draw at will. He has learned the faith as we learned it, from his catechism and from his study of theology. If he wishes to know the two sides of a dispute he must examine it as we must. When preparing to make a definition in his office of supreme teacher, he first gives the matter to his theologians. They examine the sources of the doctrine in Holy Scripture and Tradition. These sources are what is called "The Deposit of Faith." The "Deposit of Faith" preserved by the Catholic Church includes: (1) Doctrines clearly taught in the Bible; (2) Doctrines obscurely taught in the Bible, and requiring the authority of the Church to decide their true interpretation; (3) Doctrines not mentioned in the Bible at all, for example: the abrogation of the Jewish Sabbath, with the obligation of observing Sunday instead; the practice of eating meat with blood, which was forbidden for a time by the Apostles (Acts 15:20). The "Deposit of Faith" is the body of truth divinely proclaimed by Our Lord through His Apostles for our belief. These truths of Revelation were complete at the death of the last Apostle – St. John – who died in the year 99 A.D. These truths, which we must believe in order to be Catholics, were all given to us by that time. The dogmas (doctrines) of the Church never can suffer change. They are today precisely what they were at the beginning of the Church. There are no new doctrines, and there can be no modification of old ones. "The doctrine of faith which God revealed," says Vatican Council I (1869-1870), "is proposed, not as a mere philosophical discovery to be elaborated by human minds, but as the *Divine Deposit delivered by Christ to His spouse* (the Church) to be by her faithfully guarded and infallibly declared."

Whenever a heretic challenged some revealed truth of the Faith, it became necessary for the Pope, either alone or together with his Bishops in Council, to re-express in more exact language the doctrine under attack, *so that never again could there be any doubt about its meaning.* This was done by definition. This does not mean that a new dogma is ever added to the Faith, or that something is added to an old dogma. It means merely that doubt or confusion has been cast on a doctrine, and it has become necessary for the Pope to remove the doubt and confusion. The theologians will find the doctrine stated either explicitly or implicitly in the "Deposit of Faith," and it is the truth either way. A doctrine is *explicitly* expressed when it is brought out definitely in words, openly, plainly. A dogma is *implicitly* expressed when it is hinted at but not specifically stated.

So a definition of a doctrine is the more precise expression of the doctrine. Its purpose is to *clarify*. In other words, a definition is the last word on the subject. Papal definition precludes any further interpretation of a dogma. The Church has taught from its beginning that no matter how much a doctrine may be developed or meditated upon, never, never can its meaning in any way be changed. Pope Leo XIII in his Encyclical "Testem Benevolentiae" of January 22, 1899 stated: " . . . That sense of the sacred dogmas is to be faithfully kept which Holy Mother Church has once declared, and is not to be departed from under the specious pretext of a more profound understanding" (Const. de Fid. cath. c. iv.).

A formula is generally used when a doctrine on faith or morals is defined ex cathedra, such as: "The most Holy Roman Church firmly believes, professes and preaches. . . ," or "We declare, say, define, and pronounce. . ." This lays great emphasis upon the statement, as did our Lord's "Amen, amen I say to you. . ." Note the formula in the proclamation of the dogma of the Immaculate Conception: " . . . We declare, pronounce and define: the doctrine that maintains that the most Blessed Virgin Mary in the first instant of her conception . . . was preserved free from all stain of original sin . . . is a doctrine revealed by God and therefore must be firmly and constantly held by all the faithful . . . "

So, when the Pope comes finally to the act of definition – when, acting in his highest official capacity of teacher of the Universal Church, he defines a point of faith or morals, with the intent of binding the whole Church – then we believe, by virtue of Christ's promise, that the decision will be infallibly right.

The Pope is also infallible when he teaches the Church as head of all his Bishops in assembly (in Council). An Ecumenical or General Council is a Council summoned by the Pope. It is made up of Bishops of the whole world, and other high ranking prelates with a right to vote. Its decrees are not binding until approved by the Pope. Only its *doctrinal* decrees, when they are confirmed by the Pope, are infallible. (Vatican Council II was a *Pastoral* Council, not a Doctrinal Council, and thus, none of its decrees are in themselves infallible.) The Pope is also infallible when he acts singly, by himself, as the head of the Church – provided he makes it clear that he is speaking ex cathedra (from the Chair of Peter) in defining a dogma, of faith or morals, for the whole Church.

A Papal Encyclical or Allocution is not an instrument of *definition*. These documents may speak on the subject of a doctrine of the Church though; and, if so, what is expounded by the Pope in them does demand consent *if they reiterate Catholic doctrine*. (The value of Tradition is such that even the Encyclicals and other documents of the ordinary teaching of the Sovereign Pontiff are infallible *only when the teachings are confirmed by Tradition*.) There actually have been times in the history of the Church when the Pope, speaking unthinkingly and from his first hasty judgment (and not ex cathedra), has erred in a matter of doctrine. Pope John XXII made just such a mistake, and it was the people who discovered it, and called it to his attention. He investigated the matter, acknowledged his misconception, and corrected his statement. The Holy Ghost will not allow error in Faith or morals to be officially taught by the Church!

The Apostles were the original teachers of the pure doctrine of Jesus Christ. Their teachings were regarded as holy and unchangeable. They insisted on unity of Faith among the Christians, and on a full acceptance of every single dogma of the Faith. St. James in his Epistle, Chapter 2, Verse 10, states: "And whosoever shall keep the whole law, but offend in *one point,* is become guilty of *all."* And the footnote to this verse, Catholic Douay Bible, states: "That is, he becomes a transgressor of the law in such a manner, that the observing of all other points will not avail him to salvation; *for he despises the lawgiver*, and breaks through the great and general commandment of charity, even by one mortal sin. For all the precepts of the law are to be considered as one total and entire law, and as it were a chain of precepts, where, by breaking one link of this chain, the whole chain is broken, or the integrity of the law consisting of a collection of precepts. A sinner, therefore, by a grievous offence against any one precept, incurs eternal punishment."

Thus, anyone who refused to accept all the doctrines of the Church, was immediately excommunicated, called a heretic, and shunned by the faithful. "A man that is a heretic, after the first and second admonition, avoid: knowing that he that is such a one is subverted and sinneth, being condemned by his own judgment" (Titus 3:10-11).

A doctrine or a dogma of the Church, then, is a truth which has been revealed by God, and must be believed by all. One cannot choose one, discard another. To say that we approve some, and disapprove others, *is to presume to stand in judgment of the truths of God.*

HERESIES IN THE CHURCH

"Heresies have often arisen and still arise because of this, that disgruntled minds will quarrel, or disloyal trouble-makers will not keep the unity. But these things the Lord allows and endures, leaving man's freedom unimpaired, so that when our minds and hearts are tested by the touchstone of truth, the unswerving faith of those who are approved may appear in the clearest light. This is foretold by the Holy Spirit through the Apostle Paul when he says: 'There must be also heresies, that those approved may be manifest among you' (1 Cor. 11:19). Thus are the faithful proved, thus the faithless discovered; thus too even before the day of judgment, already here below, the souls of the just and unjust are distinguished, and the wheat is separated from the chaff" (St. Cyprian, Bishop of Carthage, 249-258, on "The Unity of the Catholic Church" from the book ANCIENT CHRISTIAN WRITERS, page 52).

"They went out from us but they were not of us. For if they had been of us, they would no doubt have remained with us . . . " (1 John 2:19).

"When" says St. Cyprian "the devil saw that the worship of idols was abolished, and the heathen temples emptied (after Christianity was flourishing), he thought of a new poison, and led men into error under cover of the Christian religion and the poison of false doctrine . . . " The subtle and wicked doctrine which opened the way for the succession of heresies which were soon to harass the Church in the East, was an attack on the Divinity of Our Lord, Jesus Christ. Arius, a priest of Alexandria, Egypt in the Fourth Century, declared that the second person of the Holy Trinity was not equal with the Father; which was to say, that the nature which Jesus possessed in the Godhead from all eternity was not divine: Christ was not God! Arianism spread like wildfire in spite of its condemnation by the Council of Nicea in 325. Cardinal Newman conservatively estimated that *eighty per cent* of the Bishops of the Catholic Church followed Arius into heresy. "The whole world groaned to find itself Arian," St. Jerome complained. Lucifer did not stop there. The plan unfolds with startling clarity in the heresies which immediately follow. Around the year 360, Macedonius, then Bishop of

Constantinople, denied the Divinity of the Holy Ghost. In 428, Nestorius, also Bishop of Constantinople, threw all subterfuge to the winds and declared openly that Mary was not the Mother of God. He did this by making Jesus out to be not one person but two persons! In 451 the Abbot Eutyches, of Constantinople, said that Christ had only one nature – the divine – instead of two – the divine and the human; thus making Jesus out to be not true man, and therefore, not the fruit of Mary's womb. Christendom rocked upon its foundations. It was torn and bleeding and wounded. But Lucifer, in the end, had raged in vain. For, as is always God's way in times of great stress in His Church, God raised up strong men and holy women who, fortified by grace, came to her defence. These were the spiritual children of Heaven's Queen, the Blessed Virgin Mary, who, when the interests of her Divine Son and His Mystical Body are imperiled, is ever terrible as an army set in battle array. And so a veritable host of champions of the Faith arose – men who were so carried away with the love of God and ardor for the Faith that they became saints: The renowned St. Athanasius, who did battle against Arius (With so many of the faithful having followed Arius into heresy, it seemed for a time that it was "Athanasius against the world"); St. Gregory Nazianzen, who valiantly waged war against Macedonius; St. Cyril of Alexandria, who, with inimitable courage, held out against Nestorius; and Pope St. Leo the Great, who, in the name of Peter, vanquished Eutyches. Pope Leo XIII in his Encyclical Letter on the "Unity of the Church" (June, 1896), stated: "The Church . . . regards as rebels and expelled from the ranks of her children all who hold beliefs on any point of doctrine different from her own. The Arians and the Eutychians certainly did not reject all Catholic Doctrine: they abandoned only a certain portion of it. Still, who does not know that they were declared heretics and banished from the bosom of the Church? In like manner were condemned all authors of heretical tenets who followed them in subsequent ages. There can be nothing more dangerous, than those heretics who admit nearly the whole cycle of doctrine, and yet *by one word*, as with a drop of poison, infect the real and simple faith taught by our Lord and handed down by Apostolic tradition." St. Augustine notes that other heresies may spring up, to a single one of which, should anyone give his assent, he is by that very fact cut off from Catholic unity; and St. Thomas Aquinas asserts that anyone who denies a single article of faith is by that very fact excommunicated.

"Now I recall to your minds, brethren, the gospel that I preached to you, which also you received, wherein also you stand, through which also you are saved, *if you hold it fast, as I preached it to you* . . . " (1 Cor. 15:1-2).

MOST OF THE GREAT HERESIES WERE STARTED BY MEN WHO HELD HIGH ECCLESIASTICAL POSITIONS

Arius was a priest, Nestorius a patriarch, Eutyches an abbot, Luther a monk (a priest in a monastic order), and Jansenius a bishop. They are like coiners of false money who put into circulation worthless metal in the place of the pure gold of truth. They are murderers of souls, for they take men away from the road that leads to eternal life, and tempt them into that which leads to eternal death. It is of them that our Lord says: "Woe to them by whom scandals come" (Matt. 18:7), and again, "Beware of false prophets, who come to you in the clothing of sheep, but inwardly they are ravening wolves" (Matt. 7:15).

Those Catholics who place *obedience* above *doctrine* and follow their Bishops and Priests into heresy disobey God, cut themselves off from the Church, and forfeit their right to the kingdom of Heaven. The Church holds that this is misguided and sinful obedience. The people should withstand false doctrines. What is more, they should admonish the heretical shepherds. Blind obedience leads to Hell: "If the blind lead the blind, *both* fall into the pit" (Matt. 15:14).

What is now called the Greek Orthodox Church was once a part of the Holy Roman Catholic Church, but the people of the East continued to be obedient to their bishops even when those bishops had shown themselves to be heretical and had broken with the successor of St. Peter.

How, it will be asked, could the people possibly know the truth under the circumstances, if their bishops and priests did not know it? The answer is that their bishops and priests *did* know it – just as they know it today – but they deliberately chose heresy over truth for the material advantages it would bring them. Their object was not to spread the faith in its purity, but to satisfy their own evil inclinations, their pride, their sensual desires, or their love of money or popularity. Their religious teaching was only a cloak for their vices. *In any and all events they did not truly love Jesus Christ, for Jesus says, "He who loves Me keeps My words"* (John 14:15).

But how could the people know that they should not trust their shepherds? Was it not touching that they should obey? The answer is "No"! The lukewarm, indifferent, and those who were lazy in their faith did not recognize heresy, even when it affected them and their eternal destiny. They did not *deserve* to know, because they did not *desire* to know. In days like ours, when error is so pretentious and aggressive, every one needs to be completely armed with sound knowledge, since an important part of the fray must be borne by the laity, and woe to them if they are not well prepared. *"Therefore My people are led away captive because they had not knowledge"* (Is. 5:13).

THE ORDER OF OBEDIENCE

St. Ignatius Loyola, in the first of six volumes of the Spanish editions of his letters to the Society of Jesus in Portugal, says: "Obedience is not blind, inasmuch as it clearly sees the nature of the superior's command or desire and also sees that sin is excluded. Hence blind obedience always sees that the command is morally good." And again, "We should entirely conform our will and judgment to that of the superior, wherever no sin is discerned."

St. Thomas Aquinas in his SUMMA THEOLOGICA, Secunda Secundae, Question 104, Article 5, denotes three kinds of obedience: "Accordingly we may distinguish a threefold obedience; one, sufficient for salvation, and consisting in obeying when one is bound to obey; secondly, perfect obedience, which obeys in all things lawful; thirdly, indiscreet obedience, which obeys even in matters unlawful . . . (Moreover), it is written (Acts 5:29): 'We ought to obey God rather than men.' Therefore superiors are not to be obeyed in all things."

In THE BOOK OF DESTINY – AN INTERPRETATION OF THE APOCALYPSE, by Father H. B. Kramer (Imprimatur January, 1956), Father Kramer states that "Satan will probably, through the evil world powers of the time, enforce the acceptance of unchristian morals, false doctrines, compromise with error. Through false doctrines and principles, Satan will mislead the clergy. Satan can vent more malice against the Church indirectly through bishops and priests than by his own power." And St. Pius X said: "A holy priest makes a holy people, and a priest who is not holy is not only useless, he is harmful to the world."

HAVE THERE NOT BEEN A FEW POPES WHO HAVE BEEN WICKED?

Yes, there have been. An elective monarchy, the Papacy attracted the ambition of worldly ecclesiastics and, for a time during the Middle Ages, became a prize for which rival monarchs intrigued, each trying to secure it for his own minion. Hence we find that there have been some few Popes incompetent and even wicked. Disastrous schisms have also occurred from time to time. (Schism is the action whereby one separates oneself from the Catholic Church by refusing to recognize the authority of the Pope.) The year 1054 is the date when the Eastern Christians (Near East) when into schism. This schism still exists – Greek Orthodox Church, Russian Orthodox Church, etc. In 1378 the Great Western Schism occurred in the Church, rival claimants to the Papacy sundering its unity. This schism endured until 1415. Any one of these schisms, any one of these Popes – if he had held a secular throne and were equally unfit for his office – would have brought the most powerful dynasty crashing to the ground. Moreover, the Papacy was threatened with another and, perhaps, greater, danger – the danger arising from ordinary human infirmity – for the Pope as a teacher, when not exercising his gift of infallibility, is liable to the errors of common men as we have already shown. We may, indeed, admit that, in the long history of the Papacy, there have been errors of policy, weaknesses, and wickedness which would have cost a *temporal* monarch his throne.

Because of these weak or bad Popes, the opponents of the Papacy conclude that the Papacy itself cannot be a Divine institution. But there were some very bad men among the high priests of the *Old Law* too, and yet no one contests their office of high priest as a *Divine* institution. The successors of St. Peter are frail human beings, just as *St. Peter himself was*, since the Primacy does not confer the prerogative of sinlessness or bravery. If among the 266 Popes who have ruled the Church up to our time, there were some whose lives were scandalous, God no doubt permitted this in order to show that *He Himself* rules the Church through the Popes; for not one of these so called "bad Popes" taught a single false doctrine or promulgated an ecclesiastical law that is morally reprehensible.

HAS THE CATHOLIC CHURCH HAD
MANY SAINTLY PONTIFFS?

The first 56 Popes were proclaimed saints. The first 31 of these were martyred for the Faith, yet the Papacy went on. This was a miracle of miracles! The Catholic Faith was completely spread in the early ages of Christianity by the shedding of the blood of martyrs. From the year 33 to the year 306, there were eleven million Catholics martyred for the Faith. There have been 266 Popes in unbroken succession from St. Peter to Pope John Paul II. A total of 90 of these have been declared saints. For the last century and a half the throne of Peter has been occupied the majority of the time by great men, and by good men, by several geniuses, and by one canonized saint. The names and glories of Venerable Pius IX, Leo XIII, St. Pius X and Pius XI especially stand out. The humble Pope St. Pius X was elected to the Papal throne in 1903, died in 1914, and was canonized a saint in 1954. After his election he fearlessly entered every department of life in order to "renew all things in Christ." At his first consistory on November 9, 1903, he said: "We are convinced that many will resent our intention of taking an active part in world politics, but any impartial observer will realize that the Pope, to whom the supreme office of teacher has been entrusted by God, cannot remain indifferent to political affairs or separate them from the concerns of Faith and Morals. One of the primary duties of the Apostolic Office is to disprove and condemn erroneous doctrines and to oppose civil laws which are in conflict with the law of God, and so to preserve humanity from bringing about its own destruction."

Pope Pius XI (reigned 1922-1939) will be remembered for his official documents on the evils of Communism. He wrote 9 official documents on the subject. In 1937 his renowned Encyclical on "Atheistic Communism" was widely acclaimed in all free nations. It is an excellent summary of Marxism-Leninism. In it he stated that: "The all too imminent danger" of our own days is "Bolshevistic and Atheistic Communism, which aims at upsetting the social order and at undermining the very foundations of Christian civilization." He characterized it as a "satanic scourge," carrying on throughout the world "diabolical propaganda." To this day, Russia continues to spread her errors throughout the world.

THE HAND OF GOD IS SEEN IN THE MIRACLE OF THE CHURCH'S STABILITY

The durability of the Catholic Church is the marvel of her enemies. It is only the hand of God that could have brought her safely through such perils which have proved fatal to merely human institutions. Often death seemed to have come upon her, but, sustained by her Divine vitality, she cast off disease as a garment, and rose from her bed of sickness. She is like the house of which Christ speaks in the Gospel: "And the rain fell and the floods came, and they beat upon that house, and it fell not, for it was founded on a rock" (Matt. 7:25). Often have her children heard the demons' exultant cry that, at last, she was overwhelmed in the wave of death. But the tempest passed, and day broke anew, and the eyes of men beheld her still firmly fixed as of old on the rock of Peter, triumphant amid the wreckage of her enemies.

"There is not," says the *Protestant* writer Macaulay (Essay on Ranke's 'History of the Popes'), "and there never was on this earth, a work of human policy so well deserving of examination as the Roman Catholic Church. The proudest royal houses are but of yesterday, when compared with the line of the Supreme Pontiffs. That line we trace back in unbroken series from the Pope who crowned Napoleon in the nineteenth century to the Pope who crowned Pepin in the eighth; and far beyond the time of Pepin, the dynasty extends . . . The republic of Venice came next in antiquity. But the republic of Venice was modern when compared with the Papacy; and the republic of Venice is gone, and the Papacy remains . . . Nor do we see any sign which indicates that the term of her long domination is approaching. She saw the commencement of all the ecclesiastical establishments that now exist in the world; and we feel no assurance that she is not destined to see the end of them all . . . It is not strange that, in the year 1799, even sagacious observers should have thought that, at length, the hour of the Church of Rome was come. An infidel power ascendant, the Pope dying in captivity, the most illustrious prelates of France living in a foreign country on Protestant alms . . . But the end was not yet . . . Anarchy had had its day. A new order of things rose out of the confusion . . . and amidst them emerged the ancient religion. The arabs have a fable that the Great Pyramid was built by antediluvian kings, and alone, of all the works of men, bore the weight of the flood. Such as this was the fate of the Papacy. It had been buried under the great inundation; but its deep foundations had remained unshaken; and, when the waters abated, it appeared alone amidst the ruins of a world that had passed away. The Republic of Holland was gone, and the Empire of Germany, and . . . the House of Bourbon, and the parliaments and aristocracy of France. Europe was full of young creations, a French empire, a kingdom of Italy, a Confederation of the Rhine. Nor had the late events affected only territorial limits and political institutions. The distribution of property, the composition and spirit of society had, through a great part of Catholic Europe, undergone a complete change. But the unchangeable Church was still there."

We may summarize the argument as follows: (1) The Papacy, the foundation on which the Church is built, is the only institution which has survived all the vast social and political changes and revolutions in the life and government of Europe since the days of the Roman Emperors. (2) It has survived in spite of persecution, and political intrigue; in spite of heresy and schism among its subjects, in spite of the worldliness and the weakness or incompetency of some of the Popes. Such a survival is miraculous. The Papacy and the Church over which it presides must, therefore, be the work of God. "The Ark of the Church may be swept by the waves, but it can never sink because Christ is there" (St. Anselm).

ON OBEDIENCE DUE THE
ROMAN CATHOLIC CHURCH

In the book "AN EXPOSITION AND DEFENSE OF ALL THE POINTS OF FAITH DISCUSSED AND DEFINED BY THE SACRED COUNCIL OF TRENT," by St. Alphonsus Maria Liguori, he states:

"A church which is not one in its doctrine and faith can never be the true church. Hence because truth must be one, of all the different churches only one can be the true one, and out of that church there is no salvation. Now, in order to determine which is this one true church, it is necessary to examine which is the church first founded by Jesus Christ. For, when the *first* is ascertained, it must be confessed that this alone is the True Church which, having been once the True Church, must always have been and must forever be. For to this first Church has been made the promise of the Savior that the gates of hell should never be able to overturn it (Matt. 16: 18).

"In the entire history of religion, we find that the Roman Catholic Church alone was the first church, and that the other false and heretical churches afterwards departed and separated from her . . . The innovators themselves do not deny that the Roman Church was the first which Jesus Christ founded. However, they say that the Roman Church was the true Church until the fifth century, or until it fell away because it had been corrupted by the Catholics. But how could that Church fail which St. Paul calls the pillar and ground of truth (1 Tim. 3:15)? No, the Church has not failed, and according to the promise of Christ it could not fail. But, pressed by this argument, the innovators have invented an answer: they say that the *visible* church has failed, but not the *invisible* church. But these doctrines are diametrically opposed to the Gospel. The innovators have been several times challenged to produce a single text of Sacred Scripture which would prove the existence of the invisible church which they invented, and we are unable to obtain any such text from them. How could they adduce such a text when, addressing His Apostles whom He left to the world as the propagators of His Church, Jesus Christ said: 'You are the light of the world. A city seated on a mountain cannot be hid' (Matt. 5:14). Thus He has declared that the Church cannot help but be visible to everyone . . . Were the Church at any time hidden and invisible, to whom would men have recourse in order to learn what they are to believe and to do? It was necessary that the Church and her Pastors be obvious and visible, principally in order that there might be an infallible judge to resolve all doubts and to whose decision everyone would necessarily submit. Otherwise there would be no sure rule of faith by which Christians could know the true dogmas of faith and the true precepts of morality, and among the faithful there would be endless disputes and controversies. 'And Christ gave some apostles, and others pastors and doctors, that henceforth we be no more children tossed to-and-fro and carried about with every wind of doctrine' (Eph. 4:11-14).

"What faith can we learn from false teachers when, in consequence of separating from the Church, they have no rule of faith? How often did Calvin change his opinions on the Eucharist! And, during his life, Luther was constantly contradicting himself: on the single article of the Eucharist, he fell into 33 contradictions. A single contradiction is sufficient to show that they did not have the Spirit of God: 'He cannot deny Himself' (II Tim. 2:13). In a word, take away the authority of the Church, and neither divine revelation nor natural reason itself is of any use, for each may be interpreted by every individual according to his own caprice. Do they not see that from this accursed liberty of conscience has arisen the immense variety of heretical and atheistic sects? I repeat: if you take away obedience to the Church, there is no error which will not be embraced."

WHO THEN CAN BE SAVED?

"Strive to enter by the narrow gate: for many, I say to you, shall seek to enter, and shall not be able" (Luke 13:24).

Isaias, the great prophet, who foretold the coming of Our Lord, and the glorious establishing and perpetual flourishing of the Church of Christ, said the elect shall be as few as the forgotten ears of corn remaining on the stalks after the harvesting. Or as few as the bunches of grapes left on the vines after the pickers have finished their work. Or as few as the olives that remain after the shaking of the olive tree. Or as two or three berries on the top of a bough (Isaias 17:5-6). And "They that remain of the trees of his forest shall be so few that they shall easily be numbered, and a child shall write them down" (Isaias, 10:19). The Cure' d'Ars (St. John Marie Vianney), a poor parish priest in France, who was canonized by Pope Pius XI, in 1925, used these texts from Isaias in his sermons over and over, in order to help his people to realize how few are saved. He used them not only as applying in the Old Testament, but in the New Testament as well, for all time. As a result, the Cure' d'Ars won hundreds of souls to God.

Before going into other statements from Scripture on the fewness of the saved, it might be well here to say a few words about Holy Scripture and its interpretation. Holy Scripture, having God for its author ("inspired of God" 2 Tim 3:16), is free from all error. Pope Leo XIII in his encyclical "Providentissimus Deus" dated November 18, 1893 stated that "All of the books that the Church accepts as sacred and canonical, in their entirety, and together with all their parts, were written under the inspiration of the Holy Spirit . . . By its very nature inspiration not only excludes all error, but makes its presence as utterly impossible as it is for God, the supreme truth, to be the author of any error whatever. Vatican Council I made the unqualified statement that the books of the Old and the New Testament . . . have God for their author. This is the ancient and continuous belief of the Church; a belief, too, that was solemnly defined in the Councils of Florence and Trent and finally reaffirmed and more fully explained in Vatican Council I . . . With His supernatural power, God so stimulated and moved men to write, and so assisted them in their writing, that they properly understood and willed to write faithfully and express suitably with infallible truthfulness all that He ordered, but nothing more. Otherwise, God would not be the author of Sacred Scripture in its entirety . . . For this reason the Fathers and Doctors were convinced that the divine writings, precisely as written by the sacred writers, were free from all error."

And Our Lord Himself declared: "Scripture cannot be broken" (John 10:35).

Holy Scripture is to be interpreted literally. Pope Leo XIII calls attention in his encyclical "On the Study of Holy Scripture" to "the rule so wisely laid down by St. Augustine – not to depart from the literal and obvious sense except only where reason makes it untenable or necessity requires." And on June 30, 1909, the Biblical Commission under Pope St. Pius X gave this response concerning the historical character of the first chapters of Genesis. Emphasis is placed on the literal sense of the passage, which may not be called into question. Question: "In particular, may one question the literal historical sense when these . . . chapters . . . treat of facts that touch on fundamental points of the Christian religion?"
Response: "The literal, historical sense may not be questioned."

With the above as a preface, following are additional proofs on the fewness of the saved:

STATEMENTS FROM HOLY SCRIPTURE ON THE FEWNESS OF THE SAVED

"Many are called, but few are chosen" (Matt. 20:16).

"How narrow is the gate and strait the way that leadeth to life; and few there are who find it" (Matt. 7:14).

"Not everyone who saith to me 'Lord, Lord' shall enter the kingdom of Heaven, but he who doth the will of my Father who is in Heaven, he shall enter into the kingdom of Heaven" (Matt. 7:21).

"And if the just man shall *scarcely* be saved, where shall the ungodly and the sinner appear?" (1 Peter 4:18).

STATEMENTS OF SAINTS OF THE CHURCH ON THE FEWNESS OF THE SAVED

St. Jerome (420 A.D.), Saint and Doctor of the Church: "Of a hundred thousand sinners who continue in sin till death, scarcely one will be saved" (Sermon 255, E.B. app.).

St. John Chrysostom (407), the "golden-mouthed" Doctor of the Church, writing about the salvation of bishops and priests, said: "I do not speak rashly, but as I feel and think. I do not think that many priests are saved, but that those who perish are far more numerous. The reason is that the office requires a great soul. For there are many things to make a priest swerve from rectitude, and he requires great vigilance on every side. Do you not perceive how many qualities a bishop must have that he may be apt to teach; patient towards the wicked, firm and faithful in teaching the word? How many difficulties herein. Moreover the loss of others is imputed to him. I need say no more . . . "

St. Thomas Aquinas (1274): "A select few are to be saved" (Summa Theo. 1a, qu. 23, Art. 7, ad 3).

St. Francis Xavier (1552), the great apostle to India and Japan, said in his Prayer for the Conversion of the Infidels: "Behold, O Lord, how to Thy dishonor Hell is being filled with these souls . . . " (See Father Francis Lasance's prayer book "With God" published by Benziger Brothers, Imprimatur 1954).

St. Louis-Marie de Montfort (1716): "The number of the elect is so small – so small – that were we to know how small it is, we should faint away with grief. The number of the elect is so small that were God to assemble them together, He would cry to them, as He did of old by the mouth of His prophet, 'Gather yourselves together, one by one' – one from this province, one from that kingdom."

STATEMENTS FROM SCRIPTURE ON NON-CHRISTIANS
(Mohammedans, Hindus, Buddhists, Jews, etc.)

"He that believeth in the Son hath life everlasting: but he that believeth not the Son shall not see life: but the wrath of God abideth on him" (John 3:36).

"I am the way and the truth and the life. No man cometh to the Father but by me" (John 14:6).

"He that believeth in the Son of God hath the testimony of God in himself. He that believeth not the Son maketh him a liar: because he believeth not in the testimony which God hath testified of His Son. And this is the testimony that God hath given to us eternal life. And this life is in His Son. He that hath the Son hath life, He that hath not the Son hath not life" (1 John 5:10-12).

"Neither is there salvation in any other (than in the name of our Lord Jesus Christ). For there is no other name under heaven given to men, whereby we must be saved" (Acts 4:12).

"Jesus answered: 'Amen, amen, I say to thee, unless a man be born again of water and the Holy Ghost, he cannot enter into the kingdom of God" (John 3:5).

STATEMENTS FROM SCRIPTURE ON NON-CATHOLICS

Christ commissioned His Apostles to "go into the whole world and preach the Gospel to every creature" (Mark 16:15), "teaching them to observe all things whatsoever I have commanded you" (Matt. 28:20). "He that believeth and is baptized shall be saved; but he that believeth not shall be condemned" (Mark 16:16). It is manifest from this that it is not enough to believe in just the *person* of Jesus Christ; we must also believe His doctrines and obey His words – those divine truths He entrusted to His Church, among which are the seven sacraments. All creatures are therefore obliged to become members of Christ's Church for "He that believeth not shall be condemned" (Mark 16:16). And "If he will not hear the Church, let him be to thee as the heathen and the publican" (Matt. 18:17). That is, he is not to be considered a Christian at all, and is therefore, *according to Christ's own judgment*, outside the pale of salvation. Remember, Christ established only *one* Church, and this one true Church is of apostolic origin; and He said: "He that heareth you, heareth me: and he that despiseth you, despiseth me" (Luke 10:16).

Christ, speaking of those who were not yet joined in the communion of His Church, but whom He foreknew would make a good use of the graces He would give them for that purpose, says, "Other sheep I have who are not of this fold, them also I *must* bring, and they shall hear my voice, and there shall be one fold and one shepherd" (John 10:16). Here he plainly declares that all those of His sheep, who are not yet of His fold, *must* be brought to it, as a necessary condition of their salvation. In consequence of this settled disposition of the divine providence, no sooner did the apostles begin to preach the gospel, than immediately "The Lord added daily to the Church *those being saved*" (Acts 2:47, Greek translation). This evidently shows that all who are not added to the Church, are out of all hope of salvation. The same was true of all souls from the time of the foundation of the Israelite religion to the time of the establishment of Christ's Church, who were not adherents of the Jewish Faith, for "Salvation is of the Jews," Christ said to the Samaritan woman (John 4:22). (You mean to say that in the Old Dispensation you had to believe in the *Jewish Faith* in order to be saved? Yes! That's what Jesus *said*, didn't He? And "He cannot deny Himself" II Tim. 2:13.)

WILL ALL CATHOLICS BE SAVED?

No! It is not enough to be a Catholic to get to Heaven. One has to be a *good* Catholic. "Many Catholics will be lost, because they are only nominal, not practical, Catholics, and because they reject some doctrines of the Catholic Church, especially such as oppose their inclinations and passions. Remember, he who rejects even *one* doctrine proposed to our Faith by the Church will certainly be lost (James 2:10), even though he should lead a good life." (From THE PULPIT ORATOR, Volume VI.)

Our Lord said, "He who believes shall be saved" (Mark 16:16). But God said many other things as well:

"If you love me, keep my commandments" (John 14:15); and "If thou wilt enter into life, keep the commandments" (Matt. 19:17).

"He that blasphemeth the name of the Lord, dying let him die" (Lev. 24:16).

"Keep you my Sabbath: for it is holy unto you. He that shall profane it, shall be put to death. Everyone that shall do any work on this day shall die" (Exodus 31:14-15).

"Know you not that the unjust shall not possess the kingdom of God? Do not err: neither idolaters, nor thieves, nor covetous, nor drunkards, nor railers, nor extortioners, shall possess the kingdom of God" (1 Cor. 6:9-10).

"A thief is better than a man that is always lying: but both of them shall inherit destruction" (Ecclus. 20:27).

"Neither fornicators nor adulterers . . . shall possess the kingdom of God" (1 Cor. 6:9). "You have heard that it was said to the Ancients, 'Thou shalt not commit adultery.' But I say to you that anyone who so much as looks with lust at a woman has already committed adultery with her in his heart." (Matt. 5:27-28). "Keep thyself chaste" (1 Tim. 5:22). "Blessed are the clean of heart for *they* shall see God" (Matt. 5:8).

"There is not a more wicked thing than to love money, for such a one setteth even his own soul at stake . . . " (Ecclus. 10:10).

"If anyone lie with a man as with a woman, both have committed an abomination. Let them be put to death" (Lev. 20:13).

"Hear me, and I will show thee who they are, over whom the devil can prevail. For they who in such manner receive matrimony, as to shut out God from themselves, and from their mind, and to give themselves to their lust, as the horse and mule, which have not understanding, over them the devil has power" (Book of Tobias, 6:16-22).

<u>And Christ's Mystical Body on earth, His Church</u> ("He who hears you, hears Me" – Luke 10:16), <u>says:</u>

"Each act of marriage must be left open to conception" (Pope Pius XI's Encyclical "Casti Connubi", December 31, 1930).

"If anyone says that the commandments of God are, even for one that is justified and constituted in grace, impossible to observe, let him be anathema" (Council of Trent, Canon 18 on Justification).

"If anyone says that a man who is justified and however perfect is not bound to observe the commandments of God *and the Church,* but only to believe, as though the Gospel were a bare and absolute promise of eternal life without the condition of obeying the commandments, let him be anathema" (Council of Trent, Canon 20 on Justification).

Therefore, although it is true that Catholics alone profess the true faith "without which," as St. Paul assures us, "it is impossible to please God" (Heb. 11:6); nevertheless, as St. James concludes: "Faith, without good works, is dead" (James 1:22:27).

"Sometimes people say 'It is better to be a good Protestant than a bad Catholic.' That is not true. That would mean at bottom that one could be saved without the true Faith. No, a bad Catholic remains a child of the family – although a prodigal; and however great a sinner he may be, he still has the right to mercy. Through his faith, a bad Catholic is nearer to God than a Protestant is, for he is a member of the household, whereas the Protestant is not. And how hard it is to make him become one!" (St. Peter Julian Eymard, 1811-1868).

GOD'S MERCY AND JUSTICE

"If the wicked do penance for all his sins which he hath committed and keep all my commandments and do judgment and justice, living he shall live, and shall not die. I will not remember all his iniquities that he hath done: in his justice which he hath wrought, he shall live. Is it my will that a sinner should die, saith the Lord God, and not that he should be converted from his ways and live?

"And you have said: The way of the Lord is not right. Hear ye, therefore. . . Is it *my* way that is not right, and are not rather *your* ways perverse?

"Therefore will I judge every man according to his ways . . . saith the Lord God. Be converted, and do penance for all your iniquities: and iniquity shall not be your ruin. Cast away from you all your transgressions, by which you have transgressed, and make to yourselves a new heart and a new spirit" (Ezechiel, Chapter 18), for "Wisdom will not dwell in a body subject to sins" (Wisdom 1:4).

TO OBTAIN SALVATION IS THE PURPOSE OF LIFE!

This whole world was made by God from the very beginning to be a world in which *salvation* is the greatest challenge. Our Lord told His Apostles: "Go forth and teach all nations." Tell them what they should be *looking for!* The one effort which a man ought to be making every moment of his life is toward the saving of his immortal soul. Everything else would take care of itself – sanity, certitude, vocation, employment, marriage, children – all would be beautifully taken care of, if the saving of his immortal soul were the first aim of every man. "Seek ye first the kingdom of God and His justice, and all these things shall be added unto you" (Luke 12:31).

WE HAVE HERE "NO ABIDING CITY" (From Lenten Conferences given by Father Bede Jarrett, O.P., at Our Lady of Victories, Kensington, England, 1932).

"We are pilgrims – travelers; we have no lasting city here; we have no home. We are urged to live, remembering that we are travellers. This will help you to explain your life to yourself. As you look at your life, perhaps it seems unsatisfactory. It has no apparent continual growth in an orderly progressive fashion. True, for life is not really a growing up, but a journey. You are a traveller rather than a growing child. You are taking a journey to life eternal. People are disappointed because they do not understand this.

"We are always planning and designing for ourselves what one day we shall do. As children we planned what we were to do when we had grown up. In youth we planned for our middle years. As we grow older it is always in the future that the great event, whatever it is, is to happen. We plan, at last, to settle down in old age. We cannot settle down. We never shall. We are *pilgrims!* . . .If you are to go on a long pilgrimage you must accommodate yourself to others. So life is an endless accommodating of ourselves to others. You say when you begin: 'This is only for a short time; later on I shall be able to organize my life as I want it.' That will happen truly, but not *here*. No one here ever really has a chance of having exactly what he wants. Only on the other side will you really have a home. We belong to a great city, but the city lies over the far side of the river. So live that you remember whence you came, and whither you journey. Keep your eyes steadily fixed on the height towards which you climb. . . .Forget the things that are behind you. . . .Strive earnestly forward. . . .Nothing here on earth can ever content us. We get past one difficulty only to encounter another. That is right and proper. Indeed, that is life! So do not expect to find here your city – the thing perfectly worked out, complete, that you desire, dream of, work for. Do not expect to be able to settle down for long to enjoy your life. The danger that assaults us is the danger that we might settle down. We are pilgrims on the march. Always beware of comfort! Beware of being content with what you have! There – ahead – is your comfort. Pilgrims, travellers, strangers, that is all we be! We seek a city, whose maker and builder is *God*, a city that is *God Himself.* We shall enter within it by His mercy. God Himself shall be our home. Cannot you be grateful for the road, though it be rough? It does all a road was ever made to do. It takes you *home!*"

Your friend

REFERENCES

HOLY SCRIPTURE, Douay-Rheims Translation

HANDBOOK OF THE CHRISTIAN RELIGION, Fr. W. Wilmers, S.J.

APOLOGETICS AND CATHOLIC DOCTRINE, by the Most Rev. M. Sheehan, D.D.

THE SUNDAY SERMONS OF THE GREAT FATHERS, translated and edited by Fr. M. F. Toal, D.D.

THE LITURGICAL YEAR, by Abbot Dom Gueranger, O.S.B.

FAITHS FOR THE FEW: A Study of Minority Religions, by Wm. Whalen

GATE OF HEAVEN, by Slaves of the Immaculate Heart of Mary, Still River, Mass.

OUR GLORIOUS POPES, by Slaves of the Immaculate Heart of Mary, Still River, Mass.

WHAT THE CATHOLIC CHURCH IS AND WHAT SHE TEACHES, by Fr. E. R. Hull, S.J.

THE BIBLE AN AUTHORITY ONLY IN CATHOLIC HANDS, by Our Sunday Visitor Press, Huntington, Indiana

THE TRUTH ABOUT CATHOLICS, by Fr. Joseph B. Ward

INDEX

OTHER TITLES BY CATHOLIC TREASURES

Haydock Douay Rheims Bible

ROSARY PICTORIALS
Touch of Grace
Portrait of the Passion
Crown of Glory

Apostolic Digest

All About Salvation

Of Mary there is Never Enough

Examination of Conscience for Adults

IMMODEST DRESS: The Mind of the Church

The Only Begotten

Natural Calamities, Divine Threats and the Four Gates of Hell

A Layman's Look at Evolution

St. Philomena - Virgin and Martyr

After the Boston Heresy Case

Order line: 800-257-4893